נשא
N a s o

Shabbat Morning Edition

Elliott Michaelson
MAJS

Copyright Information

PARASHAT NASO

Vital Statistics	
Full text reference:	*Ba-Midbar / Numbers 4: 21 to 7: 89*
The Maftir reading:	*Ba-Midbar / Numbers 7: 87-89*
Text reference for the Haftarah:	*Shoftim / Judges 13: 2-25*

For a pdf of the Mahar Hodesh Haftarah, visit our website: www.adventurejudaism.net

Note: the English retelling of the Torah is for the entire parashah, not just the Maftir. The English for the Maftir consists of the last parts of the retelling.

MY PROGRESS

Date					
Torah blessings					
Torah reading					
Torah review in English					
Haftarah blessings					
Haftarah reading					
Haftarah review in English					

Date					
Torah blessings					
Torah reading					
Torah review in English					
Haftarah blessings					
Haftarah reading					
Haftarah review in English					

BEFORE YOU BEGIN: GOOD THINGS TO ASK ABOUT THIS BOOK

Welcome to your Bar/Bat Mitzvah Survival Guide! There are some unique features about this guide that might be useful to you during your studies, such as...

What's up with the names of people and places?

Brace yourself, for what I'm about to say (or write, actually) may come as a shock. THE TORAH IS WRITTEN IN HEBREW. Big surprise, I know. So here's the issue many of my students have: in English, we call him *Moses* but in the Torah, we call him *Moshe*. The first woman on Earth is called *Eve* but in Hebrew, she's called *Hava*. The Jews were slaves in *Egypt* — or was it *Mitzra'im*? The answer is both. To try to avoid this confusion between English and Hebrew names, I've decided to stick with the Hebrew. So מֹשֶׁה is translated as *Moshe*, not *Moses*, and יְרוּשָׁלַיִם is *Yerushalayim*, not *Jerusalem*. For more on how to pronounce the Hebrew names, check out the handy translation chart on page ten.

How do you show God talking?

Many of us think of God as an inspirational force in our lives, but how many of us have actual physical conversations with God? As a kid, I was always confused by the fact that God physically speaks to people in the Torah but not to us today. When the Torah records God's "speech", we don't have to think of it as physical words all the time. Moses Maimonides was one of the greatest philosophers and teachers in Judaism, and 800 years ago he famously taught that all divine language in the Torah is metaphorical. Taking that to heart, I've done my very best to express that in my English retellings. God's "dialogue" is written in a different font and with a different tone, and I avoid using direct language like "said" or "told". So did Avraham hear the actual voice of God, or did God act as Avraham's inspirational inner voice? Both beliefs are valid, and it's something I encourage you to explore with your family and your teacher / rabbi.

In these retellings, I refer to God by two proper nouns: *Adonai* and *Elohim*. *Adonai* is God's actual, personal name: י-ה-ו-ה. You'll find it all over the place in the Tana<u>h</u> and in many sidurim. *Elohim* (אֱלֹהִים) is the Hebrew word for "God". Since the Tana<u>h</u> uses both as personal names for God, I've decided to keep the proper Hebrew terms.

What about commentary and translation?

Judaism has always accepted that the Torah text contains four layers of understanding. There's the literal, basic text that you see in front of you (peshat), but underneath the basic text are three layers of metaphorical understanding just waiting to be discovered (derash, remez, sod). You have over two thousand years of scholarship and commentary — including some great stuff being written today — to help you discover these hidden meanings. I've deliberately avoided providing them here for one all-important reason: any commentaries I select would reflect *my* perspective on the text and how it should be taught, and I want you to be free to find *your own way*. That's why I'm leaving the selection of commentary up to you and your rabbi / teacher.

Instead, I've devoted my time to a careful retelling of the Torah and Haftarah texts in English. This isn't a strict translation, but it isn't a sanitized children's version, either. My aim is to provide an English format that flows as easily as a work of juvenile literature, but which preserves the content and significance of the Biblical text. I've also included suggestions for study and analysis that are based on media literacy expectations from public school programs. These blurbs usually address social and historical questions that my own students ask because they need help understanding the ancient society that produced our sacred texts. None of this replaces Rabbinic commentary, but first you need to understand a little bit about the world of our ancient cousins. Then you can work with your rabbi / teacher to find the commentaries that speak to your own interests and concerns.

Da Links!

If you're using the ebook version of this book, try tapping the hyperlinks that appear periodically in the text. Some of them will take you to useful Google maps of many of the locations mentioned in the Torah, while others will take you the *Jewish Virtual Library* or *My Jewish Learning* to learn more about the famous people and nations from the Torah and Haftarah. Enjoy!

-- EM, fall 2015

TRANSLITERATIONS OF HEBREW VOWEL SOUNDS

(A very handy reference guide...)

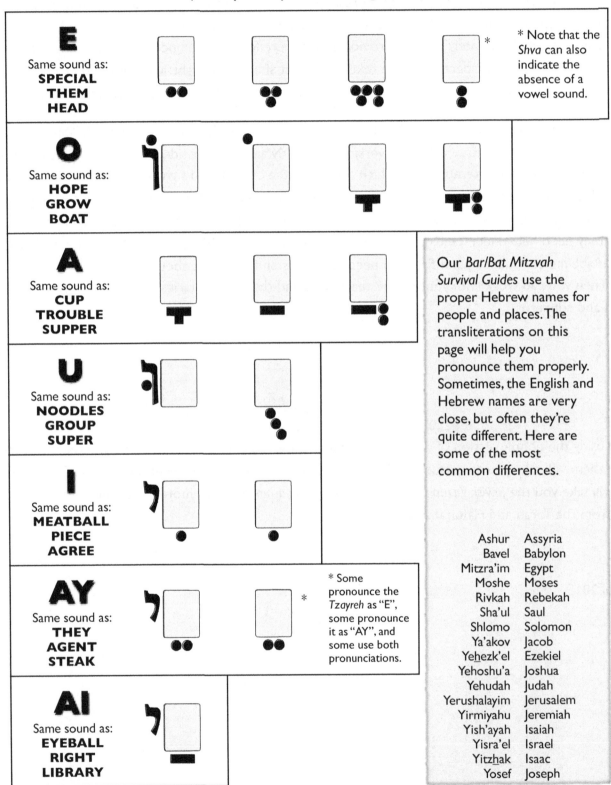

E

Same sound as:
**SPECIAL
THEM
HEAD**

* Note that the *Shva* can also indicate the absence of a vowel sound.

O

Same sound as:
**HOPE
GROW
BOAT**

A

Same sound as:
**CUP
TROUBLE
SUPPER**

U

Same sound as:
**NOODLES
GROUP
SUPER**

I

Same sound as:
**MEATBALL
PIECE
AGREE**

AY

Same sound as:
**THEY
AGENT
STEAK**

* Some pronounce the *Tzayreh* as "E", some pronounce it as "AY", and some use both pronunciations.

AI

Same sound as:
**EYEBALL
RIGHT
LIBRARY**

Our *Bar/Bat Mitzvah Survival Guides* use the proper Hebrew names for people and places. The transliterations on this page will help you pronounce them properly. Sometimes, the English and Hebrew names are very close, but often they're quite different. Here are some of the most common differences.

Ashur	Assyria
Bavel	Babylon
Mitzra'im	Egypt
Moshe	Moses
Rivkah	Rebekah
Sha'ul	Saul
Shlomo	Solomon
Ya'akov	Jacob
Yehezk'el	Ezekiel
Yehoshu'a	Joshua
Yehudah	Judah
Yerushalayim	Jerusalem
Yirmiyahu	Jeremiah
Yish'ayah	Isaiah
Yisra'el	Israel
Yitzhak	Isaac
Yosef	Joseph

PUTTING ON THE TALLIT & TEFILLIN

If you've never had the chance to put on the *tallit* or *tefillin*, this is your lucky day! Traditionally, the *tallit* and *tefillin* are worn for all weekday morning services. On Shabbat and Holy Day mornings, only the *tallit* is worn (except Yom Kippur, when we wear the tallit all day). Why the difference? There are many explanations. My favorite reason goes like this: the Torah teaches us to wear reminders of our Divine Agreement with God on our arms and our heads (i.e. *tefillin*). On Shabbat, Pesa<u>h</u>, Shavu'ot, Sukkot, Rosh Hashanah, and Yom Kippur, we perform rituals all day long that remind us of God's Agreement with us, so we don't need the *tefillin* to remind us. To put everything on, follow these basic steps. You can also find a video on our website at **http://www.adventurejudaism.net/Bar_Bat_Mitzvah_Guides.html**.

1 Recite the bra<u>h</u>ah for wrapping yourself in the tallit.

בָּרוּךְ אַתָּה יְיָ אֱלֹהֵינוּ מֶלֶךְ הָעוֹלָם, אֲשֶׁר קִדְּשָׁנוּ בְּמִצְוֹתָיו, וְצִוָּנוּ לְהִתְעַטֵּף בַּצִּיצִת.

We praise You, Adonai our God, Ruler of the universe, whose *mitzvot* make us holy, and who commanded us to cover ourselves with *tzitzit*.

2 Wrap the collar around your shoulders as if you were putting on a cape.

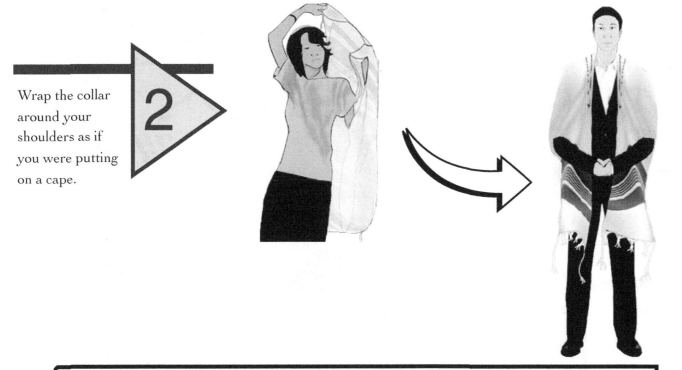

On Shabbat and Holy Day mornings, stop here!

3 Loop the *tefillin shel yad* (the one with the extra-long strap) around your bicep.

If you're left-handed, use your right bicep. If you're right-handed, use your left bicep. If you're ambidextrous like me, take your pick!

4 Before tightening the loop, recite this bra<u>h</u>ah.

בָּרוּךְ אַתָּה יְיָ אֱלֹהֵינוּ מֶלֶךְ הָעוֹלָם, אֲשֶׁר קִדְּשָׁנוּ בְּמִצְוֹתָיו, וְצִוָּנוּ לְהָנִיחַ תְּפִלִּין.

We praise You, Adonai our God, Ruler of the universe, whose *mitzvot* make us holy, and who commanded us to put on *tefillin*.

5 Tighten the loop around your bicep and wrap the strap around your forearm 7 times.

Wrap the strap around your forearm 7 times.

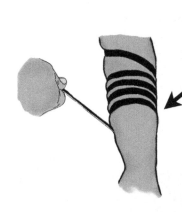

If the strap is long enough, use the extra length to keep the *tefillin* box in place on your bicep.

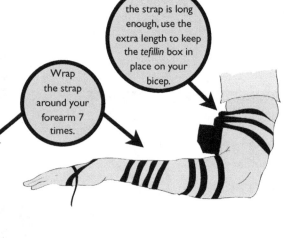

6 Place the *tefillin shel rosh* at the center of your forehead, right at the hairline.

Two long straps extend from the back of the *tefillin shel rosh*. Let them hang freely on either side of your head.

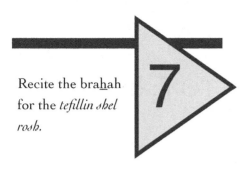

7 Recite the bra<u>h</u>ah for the *tefillin shel rosh*.

בָּרוּךְ אַתָּה יְיָ אֱלֹהֵינוּ מֶלֶךְ הָעוֹלָם, אֲשֶׁר קִדְּשָׁנוּ בְּמִצְוֹתָיו, וְצִוָּנוּ עַל מִצְוַת תְּפִלִּין.

We praise You, Adonai our God, Ruler of the universe, whose *mitzvot* make us holy, and who commanded the *mitzvah* of *tefillin*.

8 Finish wrapping the *tefillin shel yad* by winding it around your middle finger 3 times.

If the strap is long enough, you can also wind it around your hand to help keep everything in place.

Tefillin shel rosh with the two hanging straps.

Tefillin shel yad around the bicep (under the tallit.)

Tefillin shel yad wrapped 3 times around the middle finger.

Tefillin shel yad wrapped 7 times around the forearm.

You're ready to go! When you're finished, take everything off in the reverse order.

THE TORAH

BA-MIDBAR / NUMBERS 4: 21 TO 7: 89

What's the story so far?

It's been three generations since the final events of the book of *Bereshit / Genesis*. The family that began with Avraham & Sarah, Yitzhak & Rivkah, and the twelve sons of Ya'akov, Le'ah & Rahel, has now grown into the twelve tribes of Benay Yisra'el. A nation that has known great suffering, they have been rescued from slavery in Mitzra'im (Egypt) by Adonai and Adonai's appointed emissary, Moshe. Benay Yisra'el have now been living in the wilderness of Sinai for two years. Having received God's laws and *mitzvot* (commandments) at Har Sinai (Mount Sinai), they prepare for the second leg of their journey to the land of Yisra'el.

What can I expect from this parashah?

Benay Yisra'el is ready to march off to the Promised Land, but there are some logistics to take care of, first. Priestly clans need to be given their ritual assignments, rules for the *Nazir* (a kind of Israelite monk) need to be established, and a justice system needs to be set up. *Naso* includes one of the most ethically difficult sections in the whole Torah: the case of the *Sotah* (adulterous wife). One of the most famous pieces of Jewish liturgy can also be found in *Naso*. The parashah ends with a detailed account of the twelve-day opening ceremony for the *Mishkan* (portable temple). *Parashat Naso* is part two of the two-part opener to the book of *Ba-Midbar* that began last week in *parashat Ba-Midbar*.

And so, without further ado, on to the Torah!

RELIGIOUS REGISTRATION

4: 21-28
Weekday &
Shabbat afternoon
reading starts here.

A Message from Adonai came to Moshe.

> You must also count the members of the clan of Gershon aged thirty to fifty, the ones who will carry out work in the Ohel Mo'ed. When Benay Yisra'el moves from place to place, the Gershon clan will be responsible for carrying the curtains for the Mishkan and the Ohel Mo'ed, as well as the Ohel Mo'ed's animal skin coverings. They will also carry the curtains, hangings, and cords that cordon off the altar from the rest of the courtyard, along with the various tools and equipment they need to manage the rituals at the altar.
>
> All of Gershon's tasks and responsibilities will be supervised by Aharon's son, Itamar.

Ohel-Mo'ed...Mishkan: This is usually translated as "Tent of Meeting", but it wasn't like a camping tent. It was a huge pavilion for communal gatherings where the community's leaders and elders met to discuss matters of ritual and government. The *Mishkan* was the portable temple to God, while the *Ohel-Mo'ed* was the giant public space that surrounded it. To get a sense of what the *Ohel-Mo'ed* may have looked like, try going on a Bedouin camping experience the next time you visit Israel. Their "tents" can accommodate huge tourist groups for meals and for sleeping. You'll also find *Ohel-Mo'ed*-sized tents at street festivals or big weddings. The *Ohel-Mo'ed* was a special holy place like the *Kotel* or the *Bayt Ha-Mikdash* (Temple to God), so I've decided to keep the Hebrew term instead of using an awkward translation like "Tent of Meeting" or "Communal Pavilion".

15

You shall also count the men from the clan of Merari. Number off every man who is fit for service to the Ohel Mo'ed — the ones aged thirty to fifty — and organize them by family. When Benay Yisra'el moves from place to place, the Merari clan will be responsible for the Ohel Mo'ed's wood frame, cross-beams, support beams, and the pins, ropes and sockets used to fasten them together. You will provide them with an itemized list of their responsibilities.

All of Merari's tasks and duties will be supervised by Aharon's son, Itamar the Kohen.

In keeping with the Message that Adonai conveyed through Moshe, Moshe, Aharon, and the tribal leaders numbered off the clan of **Kehat** family by family. They only counted the men between the ages of thirty and fifty since they were the only ones who could take on duties in the Ohel Mo'ed. 2,750 men were counted.

Kehat: Wait... the Torah just finished talking about the clans of Gershon and Merari. What's this about Kehat? Remember that *parashat Naso* is the second half of a two-part series. Kehat's duties were outlined at the end of the last parashah, *Ba-Midbar*. When the rabbis of old divided the Torah into *parashot*, they assumed that people would come back each week to hear the next part. When you hear the Torah regularly throughout the year, ending a parashah with a cliffhanger creates a sense of continuity from week to week. It's like a really good TV series — when one episode is over, you can't wait to watch the next one to see what happens next.

To follow what's going on here, it helps to understand how the tribes were structured back in Ye Olden Dayes. It looked something like this:

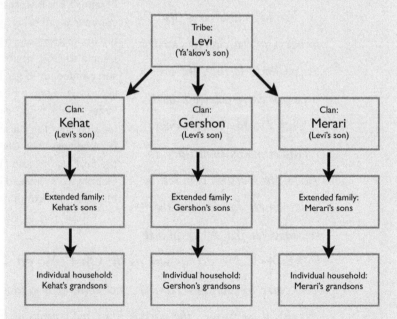

Each clan was given a list of duties, and the duties were divided up among the extended families and individual households. The duties were then inherited from generation to generation.

From the clan of Gershon, there were 2,630 men aged thirty to fifty. Their duties in the Ohel Mo'ed were assigned according to extended family groups and individual households. As for the clan of Merari, there were 3,200 men aged thirty to fifty. Their duties in the Ohel Mo'ed were also assigned according to extended family groups and individual households. Everything was done according to the instructions in Adonai's Message.

The total number Levi'im aged thirty to fifty who were counted by Moshe, Aharon, and the community leaders of Benay Yisra'el was 8,580. These men were assigned religious duties in the Ohel Mo'ed according to the commands that Moshe received from Adonai.

QUARANTINES

5: 1-4

A new Message came to Moshe from Adonai:

Command Benay Yisra'el to remove from their camp any man or woman with a skin disease, any man or woman who oozes fluids from their bodies, and anyone who has been in contact with a corpse. You will do this to prevent the contamination of their camp, since I live among them.

The people of Benay Yisra'el did so.

Many modern readers have a hard time relating to this section. In effect, the Torah describes three types of quarantine (a "quarantine" is when contagious people are removed from society in order to prevent the spread of disease):

1) People with a skin disease: in Ye Olden Dayes they didn't know much about microbiology but they did know that sick people spread infection, and skin diseases are the most visible types of infection.

2) People who ooze fluid: I know this seems kind of gross, but if you think about it, oozing pustules are also a clear sign of infection. The word זוב in this section can also mean oozing fluid from masturbation or menstruation.

3) People who touch dead bodies: in any society there are people who come into contact with corpses. If this seems creepy to us today, imagine the world of our ancient cousins, when people believed in good and evil spirits. In those days, death was often associated with evil spirits.

In the Torah, contamination can be physical (like a disease) or spiritual (like exposure to death). Physical quarantines protect our health while spiritual quarantines protect our souls. Why do you think the Torah mandates both types of quarantine? When God says "I live among them", what's the message about the importance of both types of quarantine? Your rabbi / teacher can help you explore your ideas.

FEELING GUILTY

Another Message came to Moshe from Adonai.

If a man or woman commits an injustice against another person, it is as if he or she has broken faith with Adonai. If people in this situation realize their guilt, they must admit to what they have done and repay the value of their crime plus twenty percent to the victim. If the victim is unable to accept repayment or if the victim has no family to accept repayment, the repayment is made to Adonai through the Kohen. This is in addition to the guilt offering of a ram that guilty people are required to sacrifice.

All sacred donations made by Benay Yisra'el belong to the Kohanim.

Consider this situation: you're outside on the street playing baseball with your friends. You accidentally miss the ball and it breaks the window on your neighbor's car. According to the law today, what's the consequence for breaking the window? According to the Torah's law here, what would be the consequence? Compare and contrast the two laws.

The repayment is made to Adonai…: This seems a bit strange. In Ye Olden Dayes, if the victim of a crime died, the victim's family accepted repayment on the victim's behalf. But what if the victim had no family? Does the guilty person get off without penalty? No way, says the Torah. The penalty will be paid instead to the government, which in the Torah is God and the Kohanim (priesthood). Compare and contrast this system of justice with the way we do things today.

Warning: Read this first!

The Torah includes several texts that can be ethically challenging for many modern readers and the section you're about to read is one of them. The Talmud calls it "Sotah" — when a jealous husband brings legal action against a wife he suspects of adultery. To many people today, it seems completely unfair that a husband can put his wife through this humiliating process but a wife can't do the same for her husband. As you make your way through this text, remember that the world of our ancient cousins was a very different place than ours is. Men could have as many wives as they could financially support while women could have only one husband. Inheritances were usually passed on from father to son, whereas daughters were considered part of their father's or husband's households. When a girl married, the groom's family paid a lot of money to her father's household (today we call this a dowry). Keep these ideas in mind as you read about the Sotah. Aside from issues of love and loyalty, why would it have been important for a man to be able to prove that his wife's children were really his own?

And so, without further ado, on to the Sotah…

AND SPEAKING OF GUILT... THE SOTAH

5: 11-15

Adonai brought the following situation to Moshe to pass on to Benay Yisra'el.

A man's wife is unfaithful to him and has sex with another man secretly. She is not caught in the act nor are there witnesses to the affair. Later, her husband is overcome by a fit of jealousy because he suspects his wife has been polluted by another man.

This is what must be done when a husband suspects his wife of adultery (a suspicious husband may do this even if his wife is really innocent):

The husband must bring his wife to a Kohen along with the offering of a tenth of an eifah of barley flour. This offering is used to help determine the truth, so do not add oil or spices to it as you would a religious offering.

5: 16-23

The Kohen will bring her before Adonai's Presence. He will make a cursing potion by pouring sacred water into a clay jug and mixing in dust from the floor of the Mishkan. The Kohen will uncover the wife's head and hand her the truth offering of flour while he holds the jug with the cursing potion of bitter water. He will make her take an oath by pronouncing to her:

Keep in mind the questions from the "Warning" section above. Aside from issues of love and loyalty, why might the husband be so concerned about his wife having sex with another man?

Eifah: This was an ancient unit of measurement. It was around 36 liters or quarts.

Cursing Potion: We seem to be witnessing a bit of ancient magic here. The Kohen doesn't simply "ask" God whether the wife is guilty or not. He has to go through a complicated process involving curses and signs. This was how our ancient cousins sometimes went about the business of learning the truth in legal cases. No lawyers or juries — just the accuser, the defendant, and God (via the Kohen). If this seems very quaint and superstitious, think again! In many courts of law today, witnesses are required to swear on a Bible that their testimony is true. Your rabbi / teacher can help you to explore the ways in which the Torah provides insight into the origins of modern customs.

"If no man has had sexual relations with you, if you have truly not become polluted while married to your husband, may you be free from the curse that is caused by this bitter

water. But if you have become polluted while married to your husband, if another man has indeed had sexual relations with you, may Adonai make you cursed among your people! May this water enter your body and cause your genitals to shrivel up and your womb to swell!"

The wife will reply: "Amen, amen!"

The Kohen will write this curse on a scroll and dissolve the ink in the water.

5: 24-31

The Kohen will then take the flour from the woman, hold it up before Adonai, and lay it on the altar. He will take a handful of this truth-offering and burn it up on the altar, and then he will make the wife drink the cursing potion. If she has truly become polluted by being unfaithful to her husband, the potion will become bitter. Her womb will swell, her genitals will shrivel up and she will become cursed among her people. If, however, she has not been polluted — if she has remained pure — she will be acquitted of all guilt and will be able to have children.

Genitals to shrivel...womb to swell...: Whoa, what a terrifying punishment! Of all the possible consequences for having an affair, why this? Justice is a kind of balancing act. We saw in the previous chapter that if someone causes injury or damage accidentally, the punishment is to pay back the value of the injury or damage plus a little extra for pain, suffering, etc. The punishment fits the crime. How does the punishment fit the crime in the case of the Sotah? Hint: it has to do with the body part the woman used to commit adultery.

She will suffer...her husband will be clear...: This part angers many people. Punishing the wife for her adultery makes sense, but if she's innocent, shouldn't the husband be punished for putting her through this ordeal? To many people this is plainly unfair. The Torah's main concern is the paternity of a woman's children and a husband's "right" to establish that he is indeed the biological father of any child his wife gives birth to. The wife's feelings and experiences aren't the focus here. Remember that basic text of the Torah is a product of the time in which it was written, so what we're seeing here is a record of the things that worried our ancient cousins. In those days there was no such thing as gender equality. This concept wasn't destined to exist for many centuries. But as Judaism developed over time, it took the lead in changing cultural attitudes toward women. Partly as a response to texts like the Sotah here, Jewish women and men were among the first leaders in movements that brought equal rights to women and minorities all over the world. Today, women in the great majority of Jewish communities enjoy complete equality. A lot of good has come out of responses to texts like the Sotah.

This is the legal procedure for determining a wife's guilt if she has sexual relations with another man or if her husband suspects her of doing so. She will suffer for her guilt. Her husband, however, will be clear of any wrongdoing.

NAZIR

Moshe received a new Message from Adonai.

Tell Benay Yisra'el that men or women who choose to dedicate themselves to Adonai by taking the vow of a Nazir must give up wine, alcohol, and vinegar derived from wine or alcoholic drinks. Nazirs must also give up anything fermented with grapes. For as long as they remain Nazirs, they may not eat grapes of any kind, fresh or dried. No razor may touch their heads; indeed, their hair will grow uncut until their Nazir's vow is fulfilled.

People from the tribe of Levi were required to devote their lives to God's service. They didn't have a choice; this was their inherited role in Benay Yisra'el. But what if a non-Levi wanted to devote him/herself to God? That's what the Nazirite vow is for. Nazirs were kind of like unofficial Levi'im. They had similar restrictions in terms of their lifestyle and they fulfilled religious duties. But unlike real Levi'im, they got to choose the duration of their service (a month, a year, etc.) and when their term was done they returned to their old lives. Nazirs also weren't considered to be professional religious leaders like Levi'im. On rare occasions, a person became a Nazir at birth. For details, check out the Haftarah.

If this seems strange, consider for a moment what you know of our communities today. We have professional religious leaders (Rabbi, Cantor, etc.) but we also have non-professional volunteer leaders who are elected for specific terms (synagogue presidents, boards, etc.) In fact, all Jewish organizations today are led by a combination of professional and volunteer leaders. Your teacher / rabbi can help you explore other kinds of modern "Nazirs".

Nazirs may not approach a dead body: This is the same restriction placed on Kohanim, and the restriction remains in place today in communities that still recognize Kohanim. Explore the connections between this restriction and the quarantines we saw at the beginning of the parashah.

Seven-day purification process: For details on the seven-day process for purifying people who come in contact with corpses, skip ahead to chapter 19 of *parashat Hukat.*

Hatat...Olah: In general, there were six kinds of fiery offerings made to God in ancient times. The עֹלָה (*olah*) was the most common type of offering. It was used every day, on Shabbat, and on the festivals as a way of approaching God and expressing one's acceptance of the divine commandments. A חַטָּאת (*hatat*) offering was different. The goal was to make amends for breaking any of the *mitzvot* unintentionally. *Hatat* offerings were also made by the Kohen Ha-Gadol (High Priest) on every festival and Holy Day on behalf of the entire community.

*Because this is a sacred vow of devotion to God, **Nazirs may not approach a dead body** for as long as the vow is in force — this includes burial for a mother, father, brother or sister. Nazirs will be sacred to Adonai for the entire duration of the vow. If someone dies suddenly in the presence of a Nazir, the Nazir must go through the **seven-day purification process** and then shave all the hair off his or her head. On the eighth day, the Nazir will bring two doves or two young pigeons to the Kohen at the Ohel Mo'ed's entrance. The Kohen will offer one bird as a **Hatat** and the other as an **Olah**. This will make amends for the grievous error of being exposed to the dead.*

The Nazir will make a new sacred vow of devotion by offering a male lamb as an Asham, and the Nazir will start to regrow his or her hair from that point on. The previous term of Nazir will be

Asham: This was another kind of offering. Often translated as "guilt-offering", the אָשָׁם was a kind of penalty or a fine. Just a moment, you say. It wasn't the Nazir's fault that someone just dropped dead! This is true, but isn't it possible to make a mistake without being at fault? Nazirs were expected to avoid exposure to corpses. Failure to do so was counted as breaking their sacred vow even if the exposure was accidental. Think about it: if you make a mistake by accident, who's responsible for the consequences? Explore your ideas!

declared void since it was cut short by the grievous error.

6: 13-21

When the Nazir's vow is over, the Nazir will bring the following to the Ohel Mo'ed's entrance as a fiery offering to Adonai: an unblemished year-old male lamb for an Olah; an unblemished year-old female lamb for a Hatat; one ram for a Shelamim; a basket with

Sacrifices to God usually involved a combination of animals, baked goods, wine and spices. It's not as if all this food was burned up and wasted. God may not be a person, but the Kohanim and Levi'im certainly were. Kohanim and Levi'im didn't own property and they weren't farmers — religious leadership was their sole responsibility. Sacrificial donations were their only means of support.

Shelamim: Yet another type of offering. שְׁלָמִים is often translated as "peace offering" or "offering of well-being". Its purpose was to express thanks or gratitude to God.

matzah made from flour and oil; wafers spread with oil; and the usual food and drink offerings. The Kohen will bring all this before Adonai and offer up the Hatat, the Olah, the Shelamim, and all of the food and drink. Then, from the Ohel Mo'ed's entrance, the Nazir will shave his or her head and drop the hair into the fire with the Shelamim. After this, the Kohen will take boiled meat from the shoulder of the ram, one cake of matzah and one wafer, and hand them to the Nazir. The Kohen will hold them up before Adonai as a sacred donation to the Kohanim in addition to the usual donations of meat from the ram's breast and thigh. After this, the Nazir may drink wine.

All this is the procedure for the Nazir. These obligations are in addition to the regular religious commitments.

PRIESTLY BLESSINGS

6: 22-27

Adonai's Message came to Moshe:

Tell Aharon and his sons that this is what they will say when they bless Benay Yisra'el:

"May Adonai bless you and watch over you!

May the light of Adonai's Face shine upon you and be gracious to you!

May Adonai's Face be lifted toward you and grant you peace!"

This is one of the most famous pieces of text in the entire Torah:

יְבָרֶכְךָ יְ-ה-ו-ה וְיִשְׁמְרֶךָ
יָאֵר יְ-ה-ו-ה פָּנָיו אֵלֶיךָ וִיחֻנֶּךָ
יִשָּׂא יְ-ה-ו-ה פָּנָיו אֵלֶיךָ וְיָשֵׂם לְךָ שָׁלוֹם

This three-part blessing is traditionally spoken by parents to their children at the start of Shabbat. Why do you think the authors of our siddur chose to use the blessing of the Kohanim for this purpose? Explore your ideas.

In some modern synagogues, the children gather on the bima on Shabbat morning while the congregation recites this blessing. Explore the connections between this new custom, the traditional blessing of the parents, and the original blessing of the Kohanim.

Your teacher / rabbi can help you explore other uses of this blessing in Jewish life.

In this way they will lay My Name upon Benay Yisra'el and I will bless them.

OPENING DAY

7: 1-5

On the day when Moshe finished setting up the Mishkan, he sanctified and **anointed** the altar, the furniture, and the various tools and utensils. Yisra'el's tribal chieftains brought an offering to Adonai on six carts, each of which was drawn by two oxen (one cart for every two chieftains and one ox for each chieftain). When they arrived at the Mishkan, Adonai approached Moshe.

Anointed: This refers to a strange ritual where olive oil is dripped over a person's head or over a sacred object. Why do this? No, Moshe isn't getting ready to cook dinner. Pouring oil over someone (or something) marked the person (or the object) as sacred to God. It was a way of showing that God had chosen that person (or place or thing) for something special. Can you think of other people who were anointed with oil (hint: you find a lot of it in the books of *Nevi'im / Prophets*, starting with *Yehoshu'a / Joshua*)?

Accept this offering and divide it among the Levi'im according to their needs when they move the Ohel Mo'ed and the Mishkan.

7: 6-11

Moshe did so. He gave two carts and four oxen to the clan of Gershon, and four carts and eight oxen to the clan of Merari (who were all under the authority of Aharon's son, Itamar). The clan of Kehat, however, received nothing since they cared for sacred objects that had to be carried by hand.

Then the chieftains presented their **dedications for the altar**.

Each chieftain shall present his dedication offering on his own particular day.

Dedications for the altar: In Hebrew, it's חֲנֻכַּת הַמִּזְבֵּחַ. Does the first word look familiar? Hint: it has to do with a certain famous Jewish winter festival. This long section describing the dedication of the Mishkan's altar is read throughout this eight-day festival. Why do you think the ancient rabbis chose to do this? Explore the connections between *parashat Naso* and this special annual winter event.

Shekels: Today, the שֶׁקֶל is the official currency of the State of Israel, but in Ye Olden Dayes is was an actual unit of measurement (roughly 9.5 to 10.5 grams or one-third of an ounce). Think of it as the Jewish equivalent to the British pound.

7: 12-17

On the first day, Nahshon ben Aminadav brought the offering for the tribe of Yehudah. The food offering of flour and oil was presented on a silver plate weighing 130 **shekels** and a silver basin of 70 shekels (measured according to the Mishkan's scale). He brought the incense in a gold pan of 10 shekels. He brought a bull, a ram, and a year-old male lamb for the Olah offering; a male goat for the Hatat; and two oxen, five rams, five male goats, and five year-old lambs for the Shelamim.

On the second day, Netan'el ben Tzu'ar brought the offering for the tribe of Yisahar. The food offering of flour and oil was presented on a silver plate weighing 130 shekels and a silver basin of 70 shekels (measured according to the Mishkan's scale). He brought the incense in a gold pan of 10 shekels. He brought a bull, a ram, and a year-old male lamb for the Olah offering; a male goat for the Hatat; and two oxen, five rams, five male goats, and five year-old lambs for the Shelamim.

On the third day, Eliyav ben Helon brought the offering for the tribe of Zevulun. The food offering of flour and oil was presented on a silver plate weighing 130 shekels and a silver basin of 70 shekels (measured according to the Mishkan's scale). He brought the incense in a gold pan of 10 shekels. He brought a bull, a ram, and a year-old male lamb for the Olah offering; a male goat for the Hatat; and two oxen, five rams, five male goats, and five year-old lambs for the Shelamim.

On the fourth day, Elitzur ben Sheday'ur brought the offering for the tribe of Re'uven. The food offering of flour and oil was presented on a silver plate weighing 130 shekels and a silver basin of 70 shekels (measured according to the Mishkan's scale). He brought the incense in a gold pan of 10 shekels. He brought a bull, a ram, and a year-old male lamb for the Olah offering; a male goat for the Hatat; and two oxen, five rams, five male goats, and five year-old lambs for the Shelamim.

On the fifth day, Shelumi'el ben Tzurishadai brought the offering for the tribe of Shim'on. The food offering of flour and oil was presented on a silver plate weighing 130 shekels and a silver basin of 70 shekels (measured according to the Mishkan's scale). He brought the incense in a gold pan of 10 shekels. He brought a bull, a ram, and a year-old male lamb for the Olah offering; a male goat for the Hatat; and two oxen, five rams, five male goats, and five year-old lambs for the Shelamim.

On the sixth day, Elyasaf ben De'u'el brought the offering for the tribe of Gad. The food offering of flour and oil was presented on a silver plate weighing 130 shekels and a silver basin of 70 shekels (measured according to the Mishkan's scale). He brought the incense in a gold pan of 10 shekels. He brought a bull, a ram, and a year-old male lamb for the Olah offering; a male goat for the Ḥatat; and two oxen, five rams, five male goats, and five year-old lambs for the Shelamim.

On the seventh day, Elishama ben Amihud brought the offering for the tribe of Efra'im. The food offering of flour and oil was presented on a silver plate weighing 130 shekels and a silver basin of 70 shekels (measured according to the Mishkan's scale). He brought the incense in a gold pan of 10 shekels. He brought a bull, a ram, and a year-old male lamb for the Olah offering; a male goat for the Ḥatat; and two oxen, five rams, five male goats, and five year-old lambs for the Shelamim.

On the eighth day, Gamli'el ben Pedah-Tzur brought the offering for the tribe of Menasheh. The food offering of flour and oil was presented on a silver plate weighing 130 shekels and a silver basin of 70 shekels (measured according to the Mishkan's scale). He brought the incense in a gold pan of 10 shekels. He brought a bull, a ram, and a year-old male lamb for the Olah offering; a male goat for the Ḥatat; and two oxen, five rams, five male goats, and five year-old lambs for the Shelamim.

On the ninth day, Avidan ben Gid'oni brought the offering for the tribe of Binyamin. The food offering of flour and oil was presented on a silver plate weighing 130 shekels and a silver basin of 70 shekels (measured according to the Mishkan's scale). He brought the incense in a gold pan of 10 shekels. He brought a bull, a ram, and a year-old male lamb for the Olah offering; a male goat for the Ḥatat; and two oxen, five rams, five male goats, and five year-old lambs for the Shelamim.

On the tenth day, A<u>h</u>i'ezer ben Amishadai brought the offering for the tribe of Dan. The food offering of flour and oil was presented on a silver plate weighing 130 shekels and a silver basin of 70 shekels (measured according to the Mishkan's scale). He brought the incense in a gold pan of 10 shekels. He brought a bull, a ram, and a year-old male lamb for the Olah offering; a male goat for the <u>H</u>atat; and two oxen, five rams, five male goats, and five year-old lambs for the Shelamim.

On the eleventh day, Pag'i'el ben A<u>h</u>ran brought the offering for the tribe of Asher. The food offering of flour and oil was presented on a silver plate weighing 130 shekels and a silver basin of 70 shekels (measured according to the Mishkan's scale). He brought the incense in a gold pan of 10 shekels. He brought a bull, a ram, and a year-old male lamb for the Olah offering; a male goat for the <u>H</u>atat; and two oxen, five rams, five male goats, and five year-old lambs for the Shelamim.

On the twelfth day, A<u>h</u>ira ben Aynan brought the offering for the tribe of Naftali. The food offering of flour and oil was presented on a silver plate weighing 130 shekels and a silver basin of 70 shekels (measured according to the Mishkan's scale). He brought the incense in a gold pan of 10 shekels. He brought a bull, a ram, and a year-old male lamb for the Olah offering; a male goat for the <u>H</u>atat; and two oxen, five rams, five male goats, and five year-old lambs for the Shelamim.

The dedication offerings from the chieftains of Yisra'el totaled 12 silver plates and 12 silver basins (2,400 shekels in all), along with 12 gold pans (120 shekels in all).

Overall, 12 bulls, 12 rams, and 12 year-old male lambs were offered for Olahs (along with the proper food offerings). 12 goats were offered as Hatats, and 24 bulls, 60 rams, 60 male goats, and 60 one-year-old lambs were offered as Shelamims. All this constituted the dedication offerings after the altar was anointed.

When Moshe entered the Ohel Mo'ed to address God, he heard the Divine Voice emanating from above the curtain that covered the **Aron** — between the **Keruvim**. This was how God communicated with him.

Aron: The אָרֹן was a large, ornate box that held the two stone tablets on which the original *mitzvot* from Mount Sinai were carved. What do synagogues use today in place of this Aron? Explore the differences and similarities.

Keruvim: These were mythical winged creatures with human and animal features. The Tanah isn't entirely clear as to exactly what Keruvim looked like, but our ancestors certainly knew. The top of the Aron was decorated with two golden Keruvim. They faced each other from opposite ends of the Aron and had their wings stretched out with the tips touching. God's Messages came to Moshe from between these two Keruvim.

Up next...

Be-Ha'aloteha! The final preparations are made, and after celebrating a last Pesah in the wilderness, Benay Yisra'el sets out for the Promised Land. But before long, the people start to complain about how much better things were in Mitzra'im, thereby prompting an angry response from Moshe and God. The parashah ends with a famous incident involving Moshe's siblings (Aharon and Miryam) and some slanderous gossip.

Blessings and the Maftir: Ba-Midbar / Numbers 7: 87-89

Before the Torah reading, recite one of the following blessings.
Your rabbi or teacher will tell you which one is appropriate for your community.

You call out:	**You call out:**
בָּרְכוּ אֶת יְיָ הַמְבֹרָךְ.	בָּרְכוּ אֶת יְיָ הַמְבֹרָךְ.
The congregation responds:	**The congregation responds:**
בָּרוּךְ יְיָ הַמְבֹרָךְ לְעוֹלָם וָעֶד.	בָּרוּךְ יְיָ הַמְבֹרָךְ לְעוֹלָם וָעֶד.
You say it back to them:	**You say it back to them:**
בָּרוּךְ יְיָ הַמְבֹרָךְ לְעוֹלָם וָעֶד.	בָּרוּךְ יְיָ הַמְבֹרָךְ לְעוֹלָם וָעֶד.
You continue:	**You continue:**
בָּרוּךְ אַתָּה יְיָ אֱלֹהֵינוּ מֶלֶךְ הָעוֹלָם,	בָּרוּךְ אַתָּה יְיָ אֱלֹהֵינוּ מֶלֶךְ הָעוֹלָם,
אֲשֶׁר קֵרְבָנוּ לַעֲבוֹדָתוֹ	אֲשֶׁר בָּחַר בָּנוּ מִכָּל הָעַמִּים
וְנָתַן לָנוּ אֶת תּוֹרָתוֹ.	וְנָתַן לָנוּ אֶת תּוֹרָתוֹ.
בָּרוּךְ אַתָּה יְיָ, נוֹתֵן הַתּוֹרָה.	בָּרוּךְ אַתָּה יְיָ, נוֹתֵן הַתּוֹרָה.
Let us praise Adonai, the Blessed One!	Let us praise Adonai, the Blessed One!
Let Adonai, the Blessed One, be praised forever!	Let Adonai, the Blessed One, be praised forever!
We praise You, Adonai our God, Ruler of the universe, Who drew us close to God's Work and gave us God's Torah.	We praise You, Adonai our God, Ruler of the universe, Who chose us from all the nations to be given God's Torah.
We praise You, Adonai, the Giver of Torah.	We praise You, Adonai, the Giver of Torah.

שלשים ומאה הקערה האחת כסף
ושבעים המזרק האחד כל כסף הכלים
אלפים   וארבע   מאות   בשׁקל
הקדש כפות זהב שתים עשרה מלאת
קטרת עשרה עשרה הכף בשׁקל הקדש
כל זהב הכפות עשרים ומאה   כל
הבקר לעלה שנים עשר פרים אילם
שנים עשר כבשים בני שׁנה שנים עשר
ומנחתם ושׂעירי עזים שנים עשר
לחטאת וכל בקר זבח   השׁלמים
עשרים וארבעה פרים אילם ששים
עתדים ששים כבשים בני שׁנה ששים
זאת חנכת המזבח אחרי המשׁח
אתו ובבא משה אל אהל מועד לדבר
אתו וישׁמע את הקול מדבר אליו מעל
הכפרת אשׁר על ארן העדת מבין שׁני
הכרבים וידבר אליו
וידבר יהוה אל משה לאמר דבר אל
אהרן ואמרת אליו בהעלתך את הנרת
אל מול פני המנורה יאירו שׁבעת

89. וּבְבֹא מֹשֶׁה

אֶל־אֹהֶל מוֹעֵד לְדַבֵּר אִתּוֹ

וַיִּשְׁמַע אֶת־הַקּוֹל מִדַּבֵּר אֵלָיו

מֵעַל הַכַּפֹּרֶת

אֲשֶׁר עַל־אֲרֹן הָעֵדֻת

מִבֵּין שְׁנֵי הַכְּרֻבִים

וַיְדַבֵּר אֵלָיו:

87. כָּל־הַבָּקָר לָעֹלָה

שְׁנֵים עָשָׂר פָּרִים

אֵילִם שְׁנֵים־עָשָׂר

כְּבָשִׂים בְּנֵי־שָׁנָה

שְׁנֵים עָשָׂר וּמִנְחָתָם

וּשְׂעִירֵי עִזִּים

שְׁנֵים עָשָׂר לְחַטָּאת:

88. וְכֹל

בְּקַר | זֶבַח הַשְּׁלָמִים

עֶשְׂרִים וְאַרְבָּעָה פָּרִים

אֵילִם שִׁשִּׁים עַתֻּדִים שִׁשִּׁים

כְּבָשִׂים בְּנֵי־שָׁנָה שִׁשִּׁים

זֹאת חֲנֻכַּת הַמִּזְבֵּחַ

אַחֲרֵי הִמָּשַׁח אֹתוֹ:

After the Torah reading, recite the following blessing.

בָּרוּךְ אַתָּה יְיָ אֱלֹהֵינוּ מֶלֶךְ הָעוֹלָם, אֲשֶׁר נָתַן לָנוּ תּוֹרַת אֱמֶת,

וְחַיֵּי עוֹלָם נָטַע בְּתוֹכֵנוּ. בָּרוּךְ אַתָּה יְיָ, נוֹתֵן הַתּוֹרָה.

We praise You, Adonai our God, Ruler of the universe,
Who planted eternal life among us by giving us a Teaching of truth.

We praise You, Adonai, the Giver of Torah.

THE HAFTARAH

SHOFTIM / JUDGES 13: 2-25

What's the story so far?

The time of Avraham, Sarah, Yitzhak, Rivkah, Ya'akov, Le'ah, Rahel, and their family has long since passed. After a long exile in Mitzra'im (Egypt), Moshe leads the nation of Yisra'el to Cana'an (Israel). Under the leadership of Yehoshu'a, they regain control over their ancient homeland and settle in tribal groups, but peace is elusive. For more than a century, the tribes squabble among themselves before choosing a king to unite them. During this time of squabbling, Benay Yisra'el are led by charismatic heroes — leaders who are inspired by God to do great things for their people. These heroes are known as *Shoftim*.

Who're Mano'ah and his wife and why are they in this book?

Mano'ah and his wife are the parents of Shimshon (Samson), who was one of the *Shoftim*. Our Haftarah focuses on his parents and his birth. We don't know much about Mr. and Mrs. Mano'ah — in fact, we don't even know Mrs. Mano'ah's name. Everything we know is included in the Haftarah here. The point of this chapter of *Shoftim* is to highlight the divine intervention that led to Shimshon's birth.

The Haftarah describes a time when Benay Yisra'el were being oppressed by the Pelishtim (Philistines). Shimshon grew up to become an important champion of Benay Yisra'el, fighting the Pelishtim single-handedly with his God-given strength. You can find his full story in chapters 13-16 of *Shoftim*.

And so, without further ado, on to the Haftarah...

OPENING BLESSING

Before the Haftarah reading, recite one of the following blessings.
Your rabbi or teacher will tell you which one is appropriate for your community.

בָּרוּךְ אַתָּה יְיָ אֱלֹהֵינוּ מֶלֶךְ הָעוֹלָם,

אֲשֶׁר בָּחַר בִּנְבִיאִים טוֹבִים,

וְרָצָה בְדִבְרֵיהֶם הַנֶּאֱמָרִים בֶּאֱמֶת.

בָּרוּךְ אַתָּה יְיָ,

הַבּוֹחֵר בַּתּוֹרָה וּבְמֹשֶׁה עַבְדּוֹ,

וּבְנְבִיאֵי הָאֱמֶת וָצֶדֶק.

בָּרוּךְ אַתָּה יְיָ אֱלֹהֵינוּ מֶלֶךְ הָעוֹלָם,

אֲשֶׁר בָּחַר בִּנְבִיאִים טוֹבִים,

וְרָצָה בְדִבְרֵיהֶם הַנֶּאֱמָרִים בֶּאֱמֶת.

בָּרוּךְ אַתָּה יְיָ,

הַבּוֹחֵר בַּתּוֹרָה וּבְמֹשֶׁה עַבְדּוֹ,

וּבְיִשְׂרָאֵל עַמּוֹ,

וּבְנְבִיאֵי הָאֱמֶת וָצֶדֶק.

We praise You, Adonai our God,
Ruler of the universe,
Who appointed good prophets,
and Who expected lessons of truth
in the things they said.

We praise You, Adonai,
Who chose the Torah,
and Moshe, God's servant,
and prophets of truth and righteousness.

We praise You, Adonai our God,
Ruler of the universe,
Who appointed good prophets,
and Who expected lessons of truth
in the things they said.

We praise You, Adonai,
Who chose the Torah,
and Moshe, God's servant,
and Yisra'el, God's people,
and prophets of truth and righteousness.

DIVINE ORIGINS

13:2-5

There was once a man named Mano'ah from the tribe of Dan who lived in Tzor'ah. His wife was unable to have children. One day one of God's divine servants appeared to her.

> **Nazir:** If a non-Levi wanted to devote him/herself to God, s/he took a Nazirite vow. Nazirs were kind of like unofficial Levi'im. Shimshon was rare because he became a Nazir by birth. For more details, check out chapter 6 of the parashah.

"I see that you are barren and that you have not had children," noted the servant, "but you will conceive and have a son, so take care not to drink any alcohol or eat anything impure. After you give birth, ensure that no razor touches his head, for the boy is to be dedicated to God as a **Nazir** from the moment you conceive. He will save Yisra'el from the Pelishtim."

13:6-8

Mano'ah's wife ran to tell him what happened.

"A man of God just came to me!" she cried. "His features were like a divine servant and I stood in awe of him. I didn't ask him where he came from and he didn't tell me his name, but he told me not to drink anything strong or eat anything impure because I'm going to get pregnant and have a son. The boy will be a Nazir from womb to death!"

Mano'ah went to consult Adonai. "My Lord," he prayed, "please send Your servant back to us to tell us what needs to be done to the child when he's born."

2. וַיְהִי֩ אִ֨ישׁ אֶחָ֤ד מִצׇּרְעָה֙
מִמִּשְׁפַּ֣חַת הַדָּנִ֔י וּשְׁמֹ֖ו מָנֹ֑וחַ
וְאִשְׁתֹּ֥ו עֲקָרָ֖ה וְלֹ֥א יָלָֽדָה׃

3. וַיֵּרָ֥א מַלְאַךְ־יְהֹוָ֖ה אֶל־הָאִשָּׁ֑ה
וַיֹּ֣אמֶר אֵלֶ֗יהָ
הִנֵּה־נָ֤א אַתְּ־עֲקָרָה֙ וְלֹ֣א יָלַ֔דְתְּ
וְהָרִ֖ית וְיָלַ֥דְתְּ בֵּֽן׃

4. וְעַתָּה֙ הִשָּׁ֣מְרִי נָ֔א
וְאַל־תִּשְׁתִּ֖י יַ֣יִן וְשֵׁכָ֑ר
וְאַל־תֹּאכְלִ֖י כׇּל־טָמֵֽא׃

5. כִּי֩ הִנָּ֨ךְ הָרָ֜ה וְיֹלַ֣דְתְּ בֵּ֗ן
וּמֹורָה֙ לֹא־יַעֲלֶ֣ה עַל־רֹאשֹׁ֔ו
כִּֽי־נְזִ֤יר אֱלֹהִים֙
יִהְיֶ֣ה הַנַּ֔עַר מִן־הַבָּ֑טֶן
וְה֗וּא
יָחֵ֛ל
לְהֹושִׁ֥יעַ אֶת־יִשְׂרָאֵ֖ל
מִיַּ֥ד פְּלִשְׁתִּֽים׃

6. וַתָּבֹ֣א הָֽאִשָּׁ֗ה
וַתֹּ֣אמֶר לְאִישָׁהּ֮ לֵאמֹר֒
אִ֤ישׁ הָֽאֱלֹהִים֙ בָּ֣א אֵלַ֔י
וּמַרְאֵ֕הוּ
כְּמַרְאֵ֛ה
מַלְאַ֧ךְ הָאֱלֹהִ֛ים נֹורָ֖א מְאֹ֑ד
וְלֹ֤א שְׁאִלְתִּ֙יהוּ֙ אֵֽי־מִזֶּ֣ה ה֔וּא
וְאֶת־שְׁמֹ֖ו לֹֽא־הִגִּ֥יד לִֽי׃

7. וַיֹּ֣אמֶר לִ֔י
הִנָּ֥ךְ הָרָ֖ה וְיֹלַ֣דְתְּ בֵּ֑ן
וְעַתָּ֞ה
אַל־תִּשְׁתִּ֣י ׀ יַ֣יִן וְשֵׁכָ֗ר
וְאַל־תֹּֽאכְלִי֙ כׇּל־טֻמְאָ֔ה
כִּֽי־נְזִ֤יר אֱלֹהִים֙ יִהְיֶ֣ה הַנַּ֔עַר
מִן־הַבֶּ֖טֶן עַד־יֹ֥ום מֹותֹֽו׃

35

God heard Mano'a<u>h</u>'s plea and sent the servant back to Mano'a<u>h</u>'s wife. This time she was sitting alone in the field. When the servant appeared, she ran to fetch her husband. "The man who came to me that day — he's here again!" she called.

Mano'a<u>h</u> got up and followed his wife. When he approached the man, he asked, "Are you the man who spoke to her?"

"I am."

"When your prediction comes true, what rules must we follow? What's to be done to the child?"

"Just do everything I said to your wife," replied Adonai's servant. "She may not drink anything that comes from the grapevine or any other strong drink, nor may she eat any impure food. Have her do everything I commanded her to do."

"Please stay with us while I prepare a young goat for us," said Mano'a<u>h</u>.

"If you make me stay I will not eat your food, but if you intend to make an **olah**, you must offer it to Adonai," replied Adonai's servant.

Not realizing that he was addressing a servant of Adonai, Mano'a<u>h</u> asked, "What's your name? When your prediction comes true we should honor you."

"Why do you ask for my name when you know it is secret?"

Olah: In general, there were six kinds of fiery offerings made to God in ancient times. The עֹלָה (olah) was the most common type of offering. It was used every day as a way of approaching God and expressing one's acceptance of the divine commandments. In our story here, God's servant is asking Mano'a<u>h</u> if he intends to offer an olah as a way of confirming the arrangement: God provides a son and in exchange Mr. and Mrs. Mano'a<u>h</u> dedicate the boy as a Nazir.

Why do you ask for my name...: Human beings weren't allowed to know the names of God's servants — this was considered private information, known only to God and to the servants. The last person to ask about a servant's name was Ya'akov at the end of a famous wrestling match. For details, see the end of chapter 32 of Bereshit / Genesis.

8. וַיֶּעְתַּ֥ר מָנ֖וֹחַ

אֶל־יְהוָ֖ה וַיֹּאמַ֑ר

בִּ֣י אֲדוֹנָ֗י

אִ֤ישׁ הָאֱלֹהִים֙

אֲשֶׁ֣ר שָׁלַ֔חְתָּ

יָבוֹא־נָ֥א ע֖וֹד אֵלֵ֑ינוּ

וְי֣וֹרֵ֔נוּ

מַה־נַּעֲשֶׂ֖ה לַנַּ֥עַר הַיּוּלָֽד׃

9. וַיִּשְׁמַ֥ע הָאֱלֹהִ֖ים בְּק֣וֹל מָנ֑וֹחַ

וַיָּבֹ֣א מַלְאַךְ֩ הָאֱלֹהִ֨ים ע֜וֹד

אֶל־הָ֣אִשָּׁ֗ה

וְהִיא֙ יוֹשֶׁ֣בֶת בַּשָּׂדֶ֔ה

וּמָנ֥וֹחַ אִישָׁ֖הּ אֵ֥ין עִמָּֽהּ׃

10. וַתְּמַהֵר֙ הָֽאִשָּׁ֔ה

וַתָּ֖רָץ וַתַּגֵּ֣ד לְאִישָׁ֑הּ

וַתֹּ֣אמֶר אֵלָ֔יו

הִנֵּ֨ה נִרְאָ֤ה אֵלַי֙ הָאִ֔ישׁ

אֲשֶׁר־בָּ֥א בַיּ֖וֹם אֵלָֽי׃

---

11. וַיָּ֖קָם

וַיֵּ֥לֶךְ מָנ֖וֹחַ אַחֲרֵ֣י אִשְׁתּ֑וֹ

וַיָּבֹא֙ אֶל־הָ֣אִ֔ישׁ

וַיֹּ֣אמֶר ל֗וֹ

הַאַתָּ֤ה הָאִישׁ֙

אֲשֶׁר־דִּבַּ֣רְתָּ אֶל־הָאִשָּׁ֔ה

וַיֹּ֖אמֶר אָֽנִי׃

12. וַיֹּ֖אמֶר מָנ֑וֹחַ

עַתָּ֖ה יָבֹ֣א דְבָרֶ֑יךָ

מַה־יִּהְיֶ֥ה מִשְׁפַּט־הַנַּ֖עַר וּמַעֲשֵֽׂהוּ׃

13. וַיֹּ֗אמֶר

מַלְאַ֤ךְ יְהוָה֙ אֶל־מָנ֔וֹחַ

מִכֹּ֛ל

אֲשֶׁר־אָמַ֥רְתִּי אֶל־הָאִשָּׁ֖ה

תִּשָּׁמֵֽר׃

So Mano'a<u>h</u> slaughtered the goat on a stone block and offered it as a fiery sacrifice to Adonai. Then, with Mano'a<u>h</u> and his wife looking on, something truly wondrous happened: as the flames lifted skyward, the servant stepped into the fire and shot up to the heavens. Mano'a<u>h</u> and his wife immediately bowed low to the ground.

"We've seen God!" cried Mano'a<u>h</u>. "We're going to die!"

Sometimes, reading the Torah without the Haftarah gives us a very limited understanding of life in Ye Olden Dayes. Often, the Torah describes how the laws worked, but the Haftarah describes how people actually lived.

Parashat Naso gives us a chance to see two women in action: the woman of Sotah from the Torah (chapter 5) and Mrs. Mano'a<u>h</u> from the Haftarah. Neither of them is given a name but they're portrayed very differently. The Torah shows us that the Law gave very little power to women suspected of adultery, but the Haftarah shows us a picture of women's authority in real life. Compare and contrast the Sotah and Mrs. Mano'a<u>h</u>. Your rabbi / teacher can help you explore your ideas.

His wife replied, "If Adonai wanted to kill us, our olah wouldn't have been accepted, we wouldn't have been allowed to witness all this, and we wouldn't have been told everything we were told!"

In time, the woman gave birth a son and she named him Shimshon. Adonai blessed him. Shimshon first began to feel Adonai's spirit while he lived in the territory of Dan between Tzor'ah and Eshta'ol.

14. מִכֹּל אֲשֶׁר־יֵצֵא מִגֶּפֶן הַיַּיִן

לֹא תֹאכַל

וְיַיִן וְשֵׁכָר אַל־תֵּשְׁתְּ

וְכָל־טֻמְאָה אַל־תֹּאכַל

כֹּל אֲשֶׁר־צִוִּיתִיהָ תִּשְׁמֹר:

15. וַיֹּאמֶר מָנוֹחַ אֶל־מַלְאַךְ יְהוָה

נַעְצְרָה־נָּא אוֹתָךְ

וְנַעֲשֶׂה לְפָנֶיךָ גְּדִי עִזִּים:

16. וַיֹּאמֶר מַלְאַךְ יְהוָה אֶל־מָנוֹחַ

אִם־תַּעְצְרֵנִי לֹא־אֹכַל בְּלַחְמֶךָ

וְאִם־תַּעֲשֶׂה עֹלָה

לַיהוָה תַּעֲלֶנָּה

כִּי לֹא־יָדַע מָנוֹחַ

כִּי־מַלְאַךְ יְהוָה הוּא:

17. וַיֹּאמֶר מָנוֹחַ

אֶל־מַלְאַךְ יְהוָה מִי שְׁמֶךָ

כִּי־יָבֹא דבריך [דְבָרְךָ] וְכִבַּדְנוּךָ:

18. וַיֹּאמֶר לוֹ מַלְאַךְ יְהוָה

לָמָּה זֶּה תִּשְׁאַל לִשְׁמִי

וְהוּא־פֶלִאי:

19. וַיִּקַּח מָנוֹחַ

אֶת־גְּדִי הָעִזִּים וְאֶת־הַמִּנְחָה

וַיַּעַל עַל־הַצּוּר לַיהוָה

וּמַפְלִא לַעֲשׂוֹת

וּמָנוֹחַ וְאִשְׁתּוֹ רֹאִים:

20. וַיְהִי בַעֲלוֹת הַלַּהַב

מֵעַל הַמִּזְבֵּחַ הַשָּׁמַיְמָה

וַיַּעַל מַלְאַךְ־יְהוָה בְּלַהַב הַמִּזְבֵּחַ

וּמָנוֹחַ וְאִשְׁתּוֹ רֹאִים

וַיִּפְּלוּ עַל־פְּנֵיהֶם אָרְצָה:

21. וְלֹא־יָסַף עוֹד מַלְאַךְ יְהוָה

לְהֵרָאֹה אֶל־מָנוֹחַ וְאֶל־אִשְׁתּוֹ

אָז יָדַע מָנוֹחַ

כִּי־מַלְאַךְ יְהוָה הוּא:

Closing Blessings

After the Haftarah reading, four blessings are recited. Note that there are choices for some of them. Your rabbi or teacher will tell you which ones are appropriate for your community.

בָּרוּךְ אַתָּה יְיָ אֱלֹהֵינוּ מֶלֶךְ הָעוֹלָם, צוּר כָּל הָעוֹלָמִים, צַדִּיק בְּכָל הַדּוֹרוֹת,

הָאֵל הַנֶּאֱמָן הָאוֹמֵר וְעֹשֶׂה, הַמְדַבֵּר וּמְקַיֵּם, שֶׁכָּל דְּבָרָיו אֱמֶת וָצֶדֶק.

נֶאֱמָן אַתָּה הוּא יְיָ אֱלֹהֵינוּ, וְנֶאֱמָנִים דְּבָרֶיךָ,

וְדָבָר אֶחָד מִדְּבָרֶיךָ אָחוֹר לֹא יָשׁוּב רֵיקָם, כִּי אֵל מֶלֶךְ נֶאֱמָן וְרַחֲמָן אָתָּה.

בָּרוּךְ אַתָּה יְיָ, הָאֵל הַנֶּאֱמָן בְּכָל דְּבָרָיו.

We praise You, Adonai our God, Ruler of the universe, Creator of all the worlds,
righteous in every generation. The faithful God Who does what God says,
Who speaks and fulfills it, Whose every word is true and just.

Adonai our God, You are faithful, Your words are faithful,
and nothing You say ever goes unfulfilled. You are a faithful and merciful God and Ruler.
We praise You, Adonai, the God who is faithful in every word.

(2)

רַחֵם עַל צִיּוֹן כִּי הִיא בֵּית חַיֵּינוּ,	רַחֵם עַל צִיּוֹן כִּי הִיא בֵּית חַיֵּינוּ,
וּלְעַמְּךָ יִשְׂרָאֵל תּוֹשִׁיעַ	וְלַעֲלוּבַת נֶפֶשׁ תּוֹשִׁיעַ
בִּמְהֵרָה בְיָמֵינוּ.	בִּמְהֵרָה בְיָמֵינוּ.
בָּרוּךְ אַתָּה יְיָ, מְשַׂמֵּחַ צִיּוֹן בְּבָנֶיהָ.	בָּרוּךְ אַתָּה יְיָ, מְשַׂמֵּחַ צִיּוֹן בְּבָנֶיהָ.
Show compassion for Tzion, for she is our lifelong home. Redeem Your people Israel soon and in our lifetime.	Show compassion for Tzion, for she is our lifelong home. Redeem her distressed spirit soon and in our lifetime.
We praise You, Adonai, Who enables Tzion to rejoice with her children.	We praise you, Adonai, Who enables Tzion to rejoice with her children.

22. וַיֹּאמֶר מָנוֹחַ

אֶל־אִשְׁתּוֹ מוֹת נָמוּת

כִּי אֱלֹהִים רָאִינוּ:

23. וַתֹּאמֶר לוֹ אִשְׁתּוֹ

לוּ חָפֵץ יְהֹוָה לַהֲמִיתֵנוּ

לֹא־לָקַח מִיָּדֵנוּ עֹלָה וּמִנְחָה

וְלֹא הֶרְאָנוּ אֶת־כָּל־אֵלֶּה

וְכָעֵת

לֹא הִשְׁמִיעָנוּ כָּזֹאת:

24. וַתֵּלֶד הָאִשָּׁה בֵּן

וַתִּקְרָא אֶת־שְׁמוֹ שִׁמְשׁוֹן

וַיִּגְדַּל הַנַּעַר

וַיְבָרְכֵהוּ יְהֹוָה:

25. וַתָּחֶל רוּחַ יְהֹוָה

לְפַעֲמוֹ בְּמַחֲנֵה־דָן

בֵּין צָרְעָה וּבֵין אֶשְׁתָּאֹל:

שַׂמְּחֵנוּ, יְיָ אֱלֹהֵינוּ,

בְּאֵלִיָּהוּ הַנָּבִיא עַבְדֶּךָ,

וּבְמַלְכוּת בֵּית דָּוִד מְשִׁיחֶךָ.

בִּמְהֵרָה יָבֹא וְיָגֵל לִבֵּנוּ,

עַל כִּסְאוֹ לֹא יֵשֶׁב זָר,

וְלֹא יִנְחֲלוּ עוֹד אֲחֵרִים אֶת כְּבוֹדוֹ,

כִּי בְשֵׁם קָדְשְׁךָ נִשְׁבַּעְתָּ לּוֹ

שֶׁלֹּא יִכְבֶּה נֵרוֹ לְעוֹלָם וָעֶד.

בָּרוּךְ אַתָּה יְיָ, מָגֵן דָּוִד.

Adonai our God,
grant us joy in Eliyahu Your prophet
and servant, and in the reign of the dynasty
of David, Your anointed king.
May he come soon and lift our hearts.
Let no stranger sit on his throne.
Let others no longer inherit his glory,
for You swore to him by Your holy Name
that his light would never go out.
We praise You, Adonai,
Shield of David.

שַׂמְּחֵנוּ, יְיָ אֱלֹהֵינוּ,

בְּאֵלִיָּהוּ הַנָּבִיא עַבְדֶּךָ,

בִּמְהֵרָה יָבֹא וְיָגֵל לִבֵּנוּ.

וְהֵשִׁיב לֵב אָבוֹת עַל בָּנִים

וְלֵב בָּנִים עַל אֲבוֹתָם,

וּבֵיתְךָ בֵּית תְּפִילָה יִקָּרֵא לְכָל הָעַמִּים.

בָּרוּךְ אַתָּה יְיָ, מֵבִיא שָׁלוֹם לָעַד.

Adonai our God,
grant us joy in Eliyahu Your prophet and
servant. Come soon to lift our hearts.
Turn the hearts of parents to their children,
and the hearts of children to their parents.
May Your House be called
a House of Prayer for all nations.
We praise You, Adonai,
Who brings peace for all time.

עַל הַתּוֹרָה, וְעַל הָעֲבוֹדָה, וְעַל הַנְּבִיאִים, וְעַל יוֹם הַשַּׁבָּת הַזֶּה,

שֶׁנָּתַתָּ לָּנוּ, יְיָ אֱלֹהֵינוּ, לִקְדֻשָּׁה וְלִמְנוּחָה, לְכָבוֹד וּלְתִפְאָרֶת.

עַל הַכֹּל, יְיָ אֱלֹהֵינוּ, אֲנַחְנוּ מוֹדִים לָךְ, וּמְבָרְכִים אוֹתָךְ,

יִתְבָּרַךְ שִׁמְךָ בְּפִי כָּל חַי תָּמִיד לְעוֹלָם וָעֶד.

בָּרוּךְ אַתָּה יְיָ, מְקַדֵּשׁ הַשַּׁבָּת.

For the Torah, for our worship, for the prophets, for today's Shabbat that
You, Adonai our God, gave us for holiness, rest, glory, and wonder:
for everything, Adonai our God, we thank You and praise You.
May the lips of every living thing glorify Your Name forever.

We praise You, Adonai, Who makes Shabbat holy.

TA'AMEI HA-MIKRA: TROP CHARTS

Let's face it: learning trop can be very difficult. Most of us are used to the idea that each musical sign represents a single tone, but with trop, most signs (*ta'amim*) represent musical phrases. To add to the difficulty, there are 28 separate trop signs — each with a unique musical phrase, and sometimes the phrasing changes depending on the combination of *ta'amim* (though very few readings contain all 28 *ta'amim*). Sure, you can find sheet music to help you out, but if you're like me and don't read music, you might wind up more confused. Oy!

I developed the charts in this section to help people like me. Most of the *ta'amim* are grouped into sequences that are used commonly in the Tana<u>h</u>. The grids enable the teacher and the student to chart the music as it goes higher or lower.

These charts have proven quite helpful with my own students. I hope you find them just as useful!

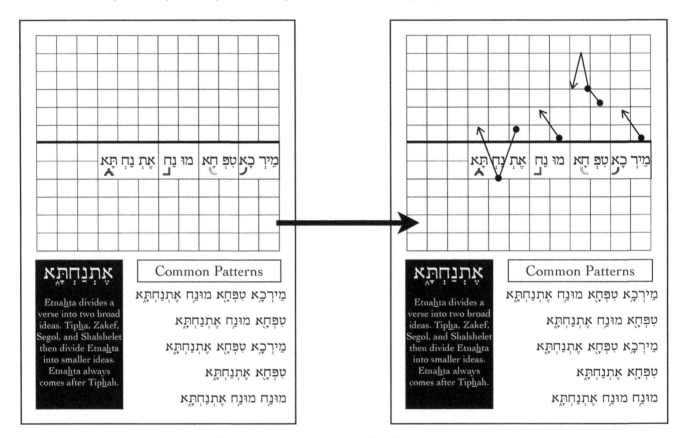

What's the point of all this trop?

Apart from musical notations, the trop (or, more properly, *te'amim*) tell us where to put the correct emphasis in each word and sentence. They also function as grammatical and syntactical notations, telling us when to pause in our reading, when to read quickly, etc. So we don't just read the punctuation — we sing it! There are seven distinct vocal systems for chanting the Tana<u>h</u>. Most people are familiar with Torah and Haftarah. See if you can find out what the other five are!

TORAH TROP

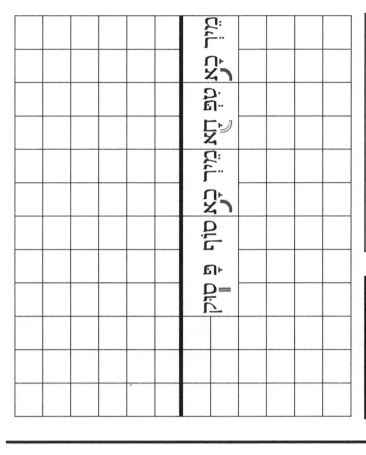

סוֹף־פָּסוּק

Sof Pasuk is also called סִלּוּק (Siluk). It marks the end of a verse. Tipha and Zakef subdivide Sof Pasuk into smaller ideas. Sof Pasuk always comes after Tiphah.

Common Patterns

סִלּוּק טִפְחָא
סִלּוּק טִפְחָא זָקֵף
סוֹף־פָּסוּק טִפְחָא
סוֹף־פָּסוּק זָקֵף טִפְחָא
סוֹף־פָּסוּק טִפְחָא

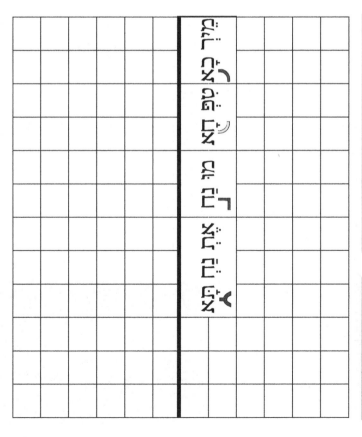

אֶתְנַחְתָּא

Etmahta divides a verse into two broad ideas. Tipha, Zakef, Segol, and Shalshelet then divide Etmahta into smaller ideas. Etmahta always comes after Tiphah.

Common Patterns

אֶתְנַחְתָּא טִפְחָא זָקֵף זָקֵף
אֶתְנַחְתָּא זָקֵף טִפְחָא
אֶתְנַחְתָּא טִפְחָא זָקֵף
אֶתְנַחְתָּא טִפְחָא
אֶתְנַחְתָּא שַׁלְשֶׁלֶת

זָקֵף-קָטוֹן

Zakef divides Etnahta and Sof Pasuk into smaller ideas, but only if they already have a Tipha. Revi'a, Pashta and Yetiv suubdivide Zakef into even simpler ideas. Zakef-Katon (a.k.a Katon) is more common than Zakef-Gadol.

Common Patterns

וַיֹּאמֶר יְהֹוָה

וְשָׂמַחְתָּ בְחַגֶּךָ אַתָּה וּבִנְךָ

וַיֹּאמֶר מֹשֶׁה

וַיֹּאמֶר יְהֹוָה ־֕ (see Yetiv card)

וַיֹּאמֶר יְהֹוָה ־֕ (see Yetiv card)

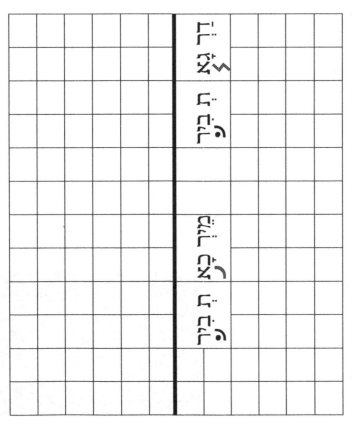

תְּבִיר

When a Tipha idea has three or more words, it needs to be subdivided. We use Tevir for this subdivision.

Common Patterns

וַיְדַבֵּר יְהֹוָה אֶל־מֹשֶׁה

וַיְדַבֵּר יְהֹוָה אֶל־אַהֲרֹן

וַיֹּאמֶר אֱלֹהִים

וַיֹּאמֶר אֱלֹהִים

וַיֹּאמֶר אֱלֹהִים

TORAH TROP

Common Patterns

זָקֵף־גָּדוֹל

זָקֵף־גָּדוֹל

Zakef divides Etnaḥta and Sof Pasuk into smaller ideas, but only if they already have a Tipḥa. Revi'a, Pashta and Yetiv subdivide Zakef into even simpler ideas. Zakef-Gadol is only found on short words and it never uses a Link.

Common Patterns

סֶגּוֹל זָקֵן

סֶגּוֹל אַזְלָא זָקֵן

סֶגּוֹל זָקֵן אַזְלָא זָקֵן

סֶגּוֹל מֻנַּח זָקֵן

סֶגּוֹל

Segol divides Etnaḥta into smaller ideas, but only if it already has a Tipḥa and at least one Zakef. Revi'a, Pashta, Yetiv, and Zarka subdivide Segol into simpler ideas. Segol never appears on the first word of a verse.

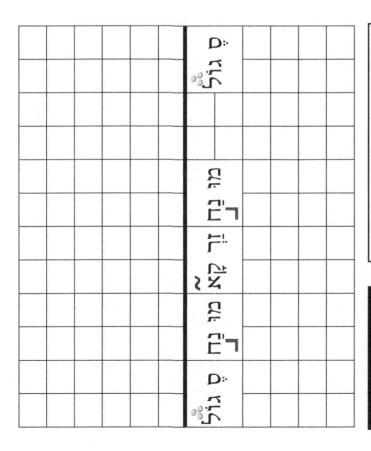

TORAH TROP

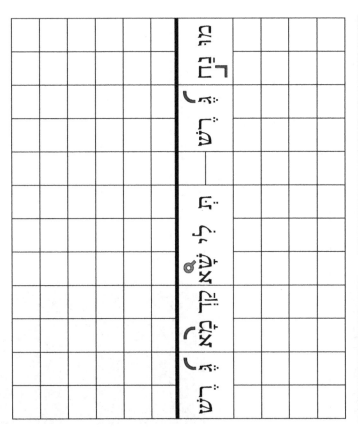

רְבִיעַ

Common Patterns

When Tipha, Zakef, or Segol need to be subdivided and they have one or two Tevirs, Revi'a is used as the Divider.

גֵּרֵשׁ

Common Patterns

If a Tevir, Pashta, Revi'a or Zarka needs to be subdivided, the subdivider is usually Geresh or Gershayim.

(a.k.a. גַּרְשַׁיִם)

48

TORAH TROP

Common Patterns

פַּשְׁטָא

Pashta is only used on the last or second-last syllable of a word. If a Pashta is needed on the first syllable, we use Yetiv, instead. Yetiv never uses a Link.

(rare)

Common Patterns

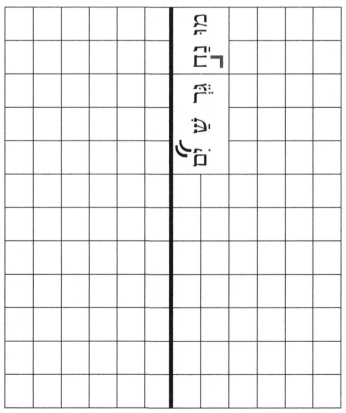

גֵּרְשַׁיִם

If a Tevir, Pashta, Revi'a or Zarka needs to be subdivided, the subdivider is usually Geresh or Gershayim.

49

TORAH TROP

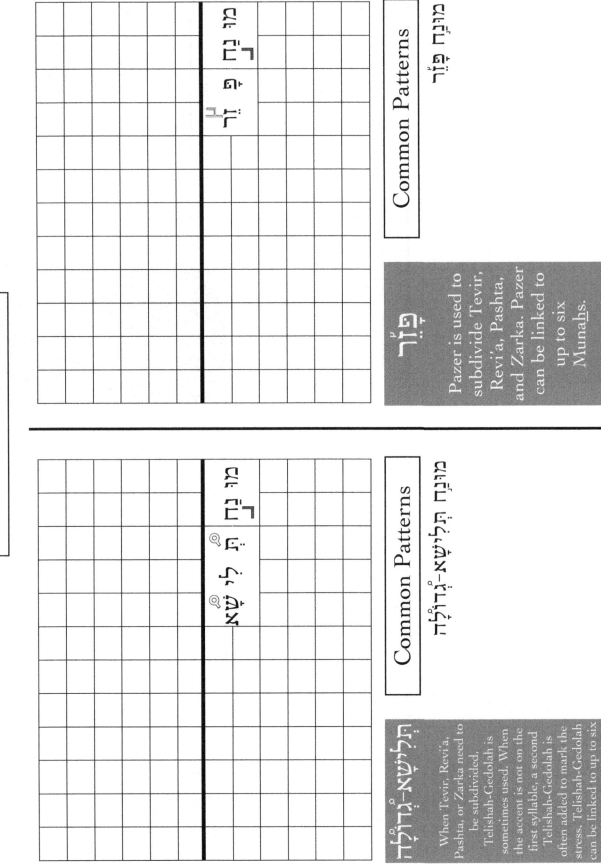

Common Patterns — מַהֲלָךְ פָּזֵר

פָּזֵר

Pazer is used to subdivide Tevir, Revi'a, Pashta, and Zarka. Pazer can be linked to up to six Munahs.

Common Patterns — מַהֲלָךְ הַתְּלִישָׁא־גְדוֹלָה

תְּלִישָׁא־גְדוֹלָה

When Tevir, Revi'a, Pashta, or Zarka need to be subdivided, Telishah-Gedolah is sometimes used. When the accent is not on the first syllable, a second Telishah-Gedolah is often added to mark the stress. Telishah-Gedolah can be linked to up to six Munahs.

HAFTARAH TROP

Top section

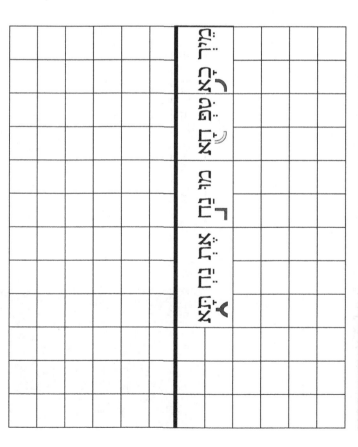

Bottom section

HAFTARAH TROP

Common Patterns

זָקֵף־קָטוֹן

Zakef divides Etnaḥta and Sof Pasuk into smaller ideas, but only if they already have a Tipḥa. Reviʿa, Pashta and Yetiv suubdivide Zakef into even simpler ideas. Zakef-Katon (a.k.a Katon) is more common than Zakef-Gadol.

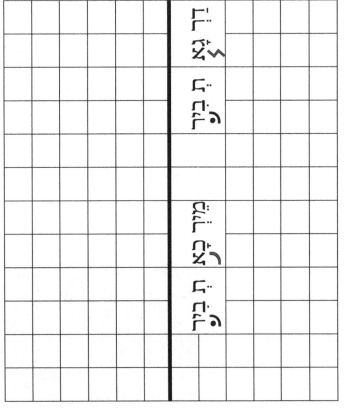

Common Patterns

תְּבִיר

When a Tipḥa idea has three or more words, it needs to be subdivided. We use Tevir for this subdivision.

Common Patterns

זָקֵף־גָּדוֹל

זָקֵף־גָּדוֹל

Zakef divides Etnahta and Sof Pasuk into smaller ideas, but only if they already have a Tipha, Revi'a, Pashta and Yetiv subdivide Zakef into even simpler ideas. Zakef-Gadol is only found on short words and it never uses a Link.

Common Patterns

סֶגּוֹל אֶזְלָא זַרְקָא סֶגּוֹל

סֶגּוֹל מֻנַּח זַרְקָא מֻנַּח

סֶגּוֹל מֻנַּח אֶזְלָא זַרְקָא מֻנַּח סֶגּוֹל

סֶגּוֹל

Segol divides Etnahta into smaller ideas, but only if it already has a Tipha and at least one Zakef. Revi'a, Pashta, Yetiv, and Zarka subdivide Segol into simpler ideas. Segol never appears on the first word of a verse.

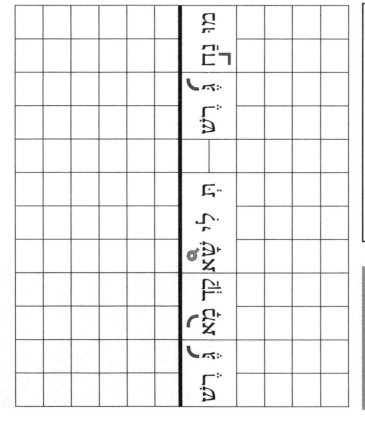

Common Patterns

Revi'a — When Tipha, Zakef, or Segol need to be subdivided and they have one or two Tevirs, Revi'a is used as the Divider.

Common Patterns

Geresh — If a Tevir, Pashta, Revi'a or Zarka needs to be subdivided, the subdivider is usually Geresh or Gershayim.

HAFTARAH TROP

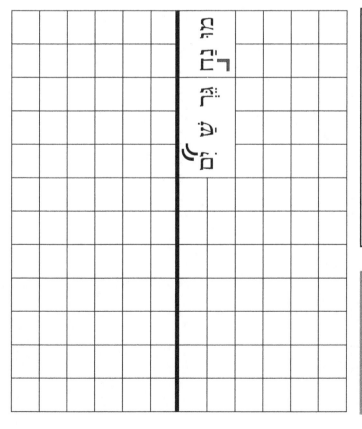

Common Patterns

יְתִיב

יְתִיב כְּטוֹב

יְתִיב קָטֹן מִטּוֹב

יְתִיב פַּשְׁטָא (rare)

יְתִיב

Pashta is only used on the last or second-last syllable of a word. If a Pashta is needed on the first syllable, we use Yetiv, instead. Yetiv never uses a Link.

Common Patterns

גֵּרְשַׁיִם

גֵּרְשַׁיִם קַדְמָא

גֵּרְשַׁיִם

If a Tevir, Pashta, Revi'a or Zarka needs to be subdivided, the subdivider is usually Geresh or Gershayim.

Common Patterns

פָּזֵר

פָּזֵר Pazer is used to subdivide Tevir, Revi'a, Pashta, and Zarka. Pazer can be linked to up to six Munahs.

Common Patterns

תְּלִישָׁה־גְּדוֹלָה

תְּלִישָׁה־גְּדוֹלָה When Tevir, Revi'a, Pashta, or Zarka need to be subdivided, Telishah-Gedolah is sometimes used. When the accent is not on the first syllable, a second Telishah-Gedolah is often added to mark the stress. Telishah-Gedolah can be linked to up to six Munahs.

D'VAR TORAH WRITING GUIDE

This guide is intended to give you a general idea of what a typical D'var Torah looks like. Yours may not look exactly like this — it will, of course, be written by you and not me! — but it should include all of these elements. As always, make sure you consult with your rabbi / teacher.

1. Don't thank people for coming — that's something you can tell your guests at the party afterwards. The person giving the D'var Torah is called a *Darshan* — literally, an "explainer". The congregation will thank *you* for explaining the weekly readings to *them*.

2. In one or two paragraphs, summarize the content of the Torah and Haftarah readings for that day.

3. Quote a verse or idea from the Torah and/or Haftarah in Hebrew and in English, and discuss its relevance in our times. This is when you bring in your own commentaries and tell us what you've learned from our ancient and modern teachers.

4. Explain how the idea you've chosen has meaning to you. You can discuss the impact the D'var Torah may have had on how you're going to lead your life, how it's affected your commitment to Judaism and its values, etc.

5. If it fits with your ideas, you may want to talk about your parents, grandparents or other family members and role models and what positive values or lessons you've learned from them. Note: this is not the same as thanking them. Save the "thank you's" for after the service!

6. Final thoughts: what does becoming a Bar/Bat Mitzvah mean to you? Why is it special to you and what have you learned in the process of studying for today? Typically, this is where you bring your discussion back to the original idea you chose from the Torah / Haftarah.

7. Your D'var Torah should be no more than four or five double-spaced pages — roughly the length of a five to seven minute speech.

My **parashah**, book from the Torah, and chapter/verse

My **Haftarah** book and chapter/verse reference....

What the TORAH says in my own words:

What the HAFTARAH says in my own words:

Questions I have about my TORAH reading, Haftarah, Bar/Bat Mitzvah process, or Judaism in general (minimum 3):	Questions my parents have about my TORAH reading, Haftarah, Bar/Bat Mitzvah process, or Judaism in general (minimum 3):

SECTIONS OF TORAH THAT STAND OUT FOR ME…

Chapter : Verse OR Section	What it says in my own words	Why it stands out for me

SECTIONS OF HAFTARAH THAT STAND OUT FOR ME…

Chapter : Verse OR Section	What it says in my own words	Why it stands out for me
↑	↑	
↑	↑	
↑	↑	

One idea or theme I want to talk about (based on my choices from charts 3 and 4):	
Verse or section from the Torah or Haftarah that relates to my theme (choose 1 or 2 from charts 3 and/or 4 and write them here):	

Commentator	The commentator's own words	What I think the commentator is trying to teach
↑	↑	
↑	↑	
↑	↑	

One idea or theme I want to talk about: (copy from previous chart)	Verse or section from the Torah or Haftarah that relates to my theme: (copy from previous chart)

Commentator (copy from previous chart)	What I think the commentator is trying to teach (copy from previous chart)	How this teaching relates to my life or the world around me
	↑	↑
	↑	↑
	↑	↑

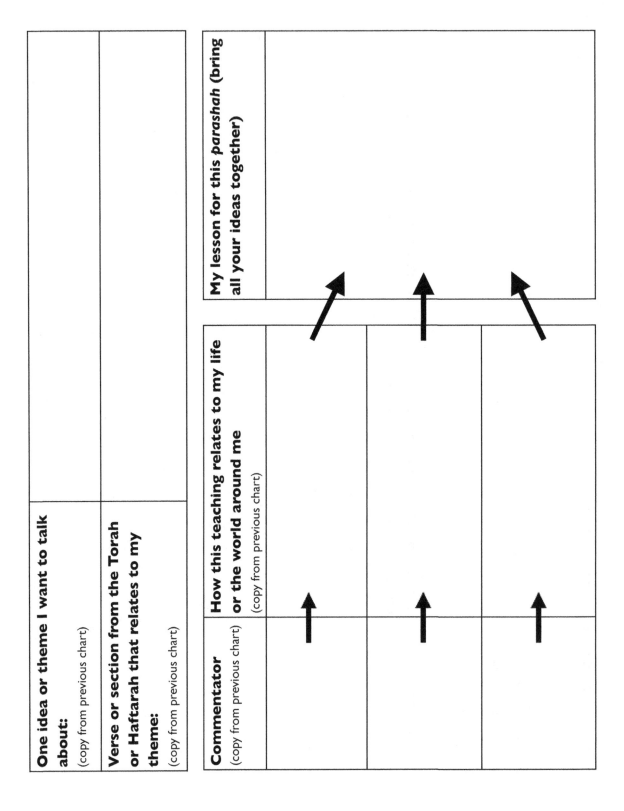

One idea or theme I want to talk about:
(copy from previous chart)

Verse or section from the Torah or Haftarah that relates to my theme:
(copy from previous chart)

Commentator
(copy from previous chart)

How this teaching relates to my life or the world around me
(copy from previous chart)

My lesson for this parashah (bring all your ideas together)

INCREDIBLY HANDY TIME LINE

The dates here are approximate. The two main columns compare the Tana<u>h</u>'s chronology with samples of writings from ancient Yisra'el's neighbors that relate to events in the Tana<u>h</u>. There are also thousands of Hebrew inscriptions and documents dug up by archeologists, but unfortunately I don't have space to mention them all! The narrow column on the left shows you when the books of the Torah and *Nevi'im* (Prophets) <u>take place</u>, **not** <u>when they were written</u>. See if you can locate your own Torah / Haftarah readings on this time line!

WHEN TORAH BOOKS TAKE PLACE	TIME LINE FROM THE TANAH (TORAH & PROPHETS ONLY)		STUFF WRITTEN ABOUT YISRA'EL BY YISRA'EL'S NEIGHBORS
BERESHIT	First Jewish family: Avraham, Sarah, Yitz<u>h</u>ak, Rivkah, Ya'akov, Le'ah, Ra<u>h</u>el, Yosef and all his brothers	**1600 BCE** 3600 years ago	
		1500 BCE 3500 years ago	
	Benay Yisra'el in Mitzra'im	**1400 BCE** 3400 years ago	
		1300 BCE 3300 years ago	
SHEMOT, VAYIKRA, BAMIDBAR, DEVARIM	Time of Moshe and the Exodus	**1200 BCE** 3200 years ago	Egyptian Pharaoh Mernepta<u>h</u> records a list of nations living in Cana'an. "Yisra'el" is included in the list (1205 BCE)
	Benay Yisra'el capture land of Yisra'el		

WHEN *NAVI* BOOKS TAKE PLACE		When Navi Books Take Place	Year	Historical Records
		Benay Yisra'el in Mitzra'im	**1200 BCE** 3200 years ago	Egyptian Pharaoh Merneptah records a list of nations living in Cana'an. "Yisra'el" is included in the list (1205 BCE)
YEHOSHU'A, SHOFTIM		Time of Moshe and the Exodus		
		Benay Yisra'el capture the land of Yisra'el and settle it.	**1100 BCE** 3100 years ago	
		Time of the *Shoftim* (tribal chiefs).		
SHEMU'EL		Time of King Sha'ul, King David and King Shlomo; First Temple is built; Kingdom of Yisra'el established	**1000 BCE** 3000 years ago	
1 MELAHIM		Kingdom splits into Yehudah and Yisra'el (922 BCE)	**900 BCE** 2900 years ago	Egyptian Pharaoh Shishak writes a victory monument about invading the region in and around Yisra'el
		Book of *1 Melahim* describes invasion of Yehudah by Pharaoh Shishak		
2 MELAHIM AMOS, HOSHE'A, NAHUM, MICAH, YISH'AYAH #1		Time of Eliyahu and Elisha; Book of *2 Melahim* describes a rebellion against Yisra'el by Mesha, king of Mo'ab; *2 Melahim* also describes war between Aram, Yehudah, and Yisra'el	**800 BCE** 2800 years ago	King Mesha of Mo'ab makes a stone monument describing his rebellion against Israel; Anonymous king of Aram makes a stone monument describing war with Yehudah & Yisra'el
		Ashur conquers Yisra'el (722-720 BCE) Books of *2 Melahim* and *Yish'ayah* describe Assyrian invasions of Yehudah and Yisra'el	**700 BCE** 2700 years ago	Assyrian kings Tiglath-Pileser III and Shalmaneser V write inscriptions and wall carvings about conquering Israel; Assyrian king Sennacherib writes inscription about his invasion of Yehudah
2 MELAHIM TZEFANYAH, YIRMIYAH, YEHEZK'EL, YISH'AYAH #2, OVADYAH		**Bavel conquers Yehudah (590's-586 BCE)** Yerushalayim destroyed (586 BCE)	**600 BCE** 2600 years ago	**Babylonians write inscriptions about their invasion and conquest of Yehudah**
HAGAI, ZEHARYAH, HABAKUK, MAL'AHI		Cyrus of Persia allows exiles to return from Bavel; Temple rebuilt; time of Nehemiyah & Ezra	**500 BCE** 2500 years ago	Persia conquers Babylon; Persian King Cyrus II writes inscription about his policy of allowing all exiled people to return home

WHEN *NAVI* BOOKS TAKE PLACE

HAGAI, ZEHARYAH, HABAKUK, MAL'AH

Events (left)	Timeline	Events (right)
Cyrus of Persia allows exiles to return from Bavel; Temple rebuilt; time of Neḥemiyah & Ezra	**500 BCE** — 2500 years ago	Persia conquers Babylon; Persian King Cyrus II writes inscription about his policy of allowing all exiled people to return home
	400 BCE — 2400 years ago	
Books of the Torah, Prophets, and other pieces of literature are edited and compiled into the Tanaḥ	**300 BCE** — 2300 years ago	Greek Empire defeats Persia and takes control of the land of Israel
	200 BCE — 2200 years ago	
Jews successfully rebel against Greek Seleucid Empire & establish kingdom of Judea (Ḥanukah)	**100 BCE** — 2100 years ago	Dead Sea Scrolls are written and hidden in caves in the Judean Desert
Time of the Mishnah (final compilation roughly 200 CE)		Roman Empire takes control of Judea
	1 BCE / 1 CE — 2000 years ago	
Jews rebel against Rome; Jerusalem and the Temple are destroyed (70 CE)	**200 CE** — 1800 years ago	**Romans build a massive arch with carvings that depict the victory over the Jews**

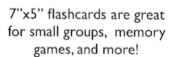

Ease your way into learning the Trop for Torah and Haftarah!

Our Trop Flashcards enhance any Bar/Bat Mitzvah study program. 28 5"x7" flashcards feature:

- the position of each ta'am in a word
- explanations that let you know what each ta'am is used for
- the most common patterns for each ta'am
- handy music charts
- a color-coding system to help students visualize the music
- suggestions for use
- terribly convenient explanatory notes and charts

Each set also includes a 12-page booklet that explains how the Trop system works.

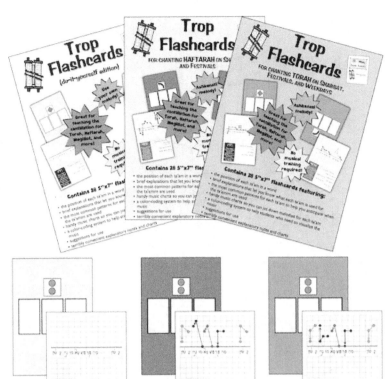

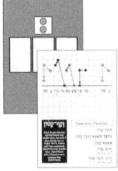
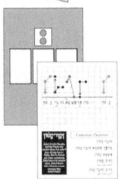

Zakef-Katon card, Do-It-Yourself edition (front and back sides).

Zakef-Katon card, Haftarah edition (front and back sides).

Zakef-Katon card, Torah edition (front and back sides).

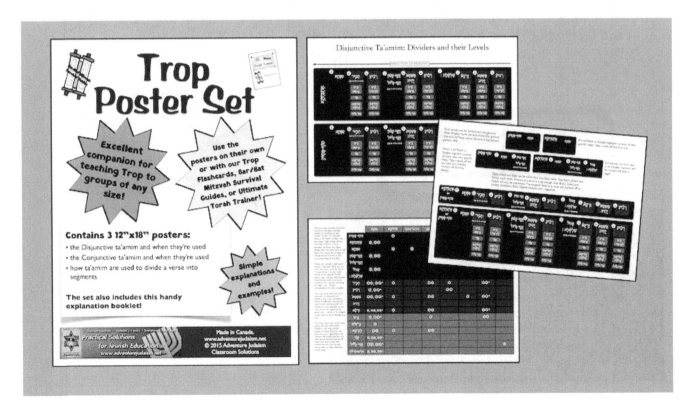

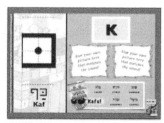

A fun way to learn about the Holy Days and the order of the Hebrew months!

The Hebrew months and Holy Days come alive with the Ḥagim & Ḥodashim Cards series. Meet any classroom or programming need with our large display cards, flashcards for small groups, or playing cards for active learning through games. Use them for:

√ **Learning the order of the Hebrew months and Holy Days**

√ **Connecting months and events inthe year to Jewish values**

√ **Designing a values-based program for the year**

√ **And more!**

The 11"x8" display cards are perfect for word walls, sorting games, class displays, and more.

The 7"x5" flashcards are great for working with small groups.

The 4"x3" playing cards are great for match games, fish, memory games, and more. Suggestions for games are included.

Made in the USA
Middletown, DE
05 May 2022